PENGUIN BOOKS

ADULT ON BOARD

Jeff and Judy Wuorio have been playing travel games as long as there have been miles of desolate highway and hours strapped in a cramped airline seat. Jeff works as a correspondent for *Money* magazine while Judy is a speech-language pathologist. When not on board something that's headed somewhere, Jeff and Judy live with their son, Nathan, in Portland, Oregon.

Adult on Board

Travel Games for Grown-ups

Jeff and Judy Wuorio

Penguin Books

PENGUIN BOOKS
Published by the Penguin Group
Penguin Books USA Inc., 375 Hudson Street, New York,
New York 10014, U.S.A.
Penguin Books Ltd, 27 Wrights Lane, London W8 5TZ, England
Penguin Books Australia Ltd, Ringwood, Victoria, Australia
Penguin Books Canada Ltd, 10 Alcorn Avenue,
Toronto, Ontario, Canada M4V 3B2
Penguin Books (N.Z.) Ltd, 182–190 Wairau Road,
Auckland 10, New Zealand

Penguin Books Ltd, Registered Offices:
Harmondsworth, Middlesex, England

First published in Penguin Books 1994

10 9 8 7 6 5 4 3 2

"The Last Word" created by Dave Silverman, appeared in *Word Ways* magazine. Used by permission of the publisher.
"Kolodny's Game" created by David G. Kolodny. Used by permission of David G. Kolodny.
"Tonto" created by Pat McCormick.

LIBRARY OF CONGRESS CATALOGING IN PUBLICATION DATA
Wuorio, Jeff.
Adult on board: travel games for grown-ups/by Jeff and Judy
Wuorio.
p.   cm.
ISBN 0 14 02.3408 X
1. Games for travelers.   I. Wuorio, Judy.   II. Title.
GV1206.W86 1994
794—dc20   93–5990

Printed in the United States of America
Set in Caslon Book
Designed by Virginia Norey

For Nathan

Acknowledgments

Many people offered suggestions and feedback as we put together the games that comprise *Adult on Board*. Thanks in particular are due Jeff Wallach, Nan Gatchel, Jeff and Kolleen Hall, the Ludlow family, David Greene Kolodny, Judy Savinar, and the Kaplan-Wilcox family of Missoula, Montana. Special thanks are due our agent, Ling Lucas, whose support and guidance have been invaluable. Lastly, our thanks to the good folks at Viking Penguin, most notably Lori Lipsky and Nicole Guisto, who have made the completion of this book an unqualified pleasure.

Contents

Introduction

> *"When I am grown to man's estate*
> *I shall be very proud and great*
> *And tell the other girls and boys*
> *not to meddle with my toys."*
>
> —*R. L. Stevenson*

They say that travel can broaden one's mind—offer new perspectives, nurture self-examination, occasionally provide a glimpse of some significant sliver of reality. It's true—just this sort of thing happened to Judy and myself not very long ago.

The only thing was, the great revelation that flashed before us was . . . well, we just had to have more toys to play with. At least on the road.

A couple of years back, we took a week's vacation in the San Juan Island region of Washington State. As was our enjoyable habit—one shared by millions of car-bound adults—we offset the droning monotony of highway travel by playing a number of word and guessing games.

However, as usual, after we'd been on the road for only a few hours, we had exhausted the supply of games that interested us. Shortly thereafter, we stopped in a bookstore in hopes of finding some new material. Seeing books of travel games only for children, we asked a salesperson if there were any that offered games more suited to adult players. Even as she answered no, the woman behind the counter grinned. "What a great idea," she said, her eyes taking on a glassy, faraway look. "My husband and I could finally leave our Trivial Pursuit cards at home."

Thus was born the idea for *Adult on Board*.

This collection is the result of our efforts to compile an array of challenging and entertaining games that adults may enjoy while getting from Point A to Point B. Although we've tried to offer as broad a mix as possible, the games do have a number of features in common. With the exception of an occasional license plate, road sign, or some sort of timepiece, the games require no equipment. Moreover, nearly all the games may be played during any sort of travel, be it by car, train, plane, ocean liner, bus, tramway, yak, or whatever.

Our title, *Adult on Board*, is misleading in two ways. For one thing, most of these games are as enjoyable on a porch as they are in a Porsche, so don't limit yourself to playing them only on the road. Secondly, most of the games are not meant to exclude children— many have simple versions that allow kids to join in on the fun.

Keeping that tie to children is important, because *Adult on Board* is basically an exercise in promoting childish fun in a grown-up way. The adult world is ridiculously strained, burdened with blackened day planners and telephones that intrude into our most private corners, not to mention those meals that mysteriously warrant a "power" label. Along the way, we've all lost sight of what becomes of Jack when his hours are filled with nothing but stacks of unanswered faxes and mounds of "While You Were Out" notes. It's an unfortunate oversight that the German poet Heinrich Heine reconginzed more than a century before anyone ever shrieked about "file not found" on a computer screen or the hour-long backup on the interstate: "Anyone who regards games simply as games and takes work too seriously has grasped little of either."

Whether you're locked in a traffic jam, weary of the in-flight magazine, or just looking for a little fun wherever you happen to be, we hope this collection will help you enjoy. Meddle away.

—Jeff and Judy Wuorio

A Couple of Quick Suggestions

"Shakespeare was wrong. To play or not to play: that is the real question."

—Dr. George Sheehan

Each listing in *Adult on Board* is self-explanatory as to how the game is played and other guidelines designed to make your play challenging and enjoyable. However, those rules are not etched in stone—by all means forge ahead if bending or changing a rule seems to make a game play better. In addition, please let us know if you come across a variation to a game that's new and different or you have any other suggestions as to how these games can be made even better. Use the address at the back of the book to do just that. How's that for interactive democracy? Did your gym teacher have a suggestion box in the corner where the dodge balls were kept? We think not.

Wordplay Games

> "A pun is a noble thing per se. It fills
> the mind; it is as perfect as a sonnet;
> better."
>
> —Charles Lamb

> "Punning is a low species of wit."
>
> —Noah Webster

Alpha-Blab

This game, suggested by our friends Jeff and Kolleen Hall, is based on an actors' exercise that teaches improvisational skills.

❏ **Aim of the Game:** To start and maintain a conversation in which the first letter of the first word in each sentence follows an alphabetical order.

❏ **Number of Players:** Two or more.

❏ **Game Plan:** The first player starts the game with the phrase, "All right, here we go." Since that starts with the letter *A,* the next player must follow with a sentence beginning with the letter *B.* The second sentence must somehow make sense in the context of the first sentence. The third sentence must begin with a *C,* and so on.

Here's an example:
- **Player #1:** All right, here we go.
- **Player #2:** Beautiful weather today, just beautiful.
- **Player #3:** Couldn't we do be doing something else to take advantage of the nice weather?
- **Player #4:** Do you have a suggestion?
- **Player #1:** Everything sounds good to me.
- **Player #2:** Flying a kite is one possibility.

- **Player #3:** Going downtown is another.
- **Player #4:** Have you seen the new exhibit at the museum?

Note how certain letters allow for subject changes. That's perfectly okay, just so long as the sentence sounds like a part of a normal conversation.

❑ **How To Win:** Players drop from the game as they're unable to add a sentence. The last player remaining is the winner. Like the exercise that spawned Alpha-Blab, however, it's also a lot of fun to leave the competition out and see how long you can keep going.

❑ **Suggestions For Play:** Similar to other games that test players' ability to improvise, this is a good game in which to impose a time limit—30 seconds is a good starting point, but feel free to adjust that to suit your taste.

Author! Author!

Most of us will never come close to crafting the Great American Novel, but this at least gives us a chance to create some great writers. Cheer up—this takes a lot less time.

❑ **Aim of the Game:** To devise writers' "names" that match book titles.

❑ **Number of Players:** One or more.

❑ **Game Plan:**   In multiplayer games, participants first agree on a book category—in this instance, let's say cookbooks. In turn, players then think of a book title and an author's name that somehow puns the title. Players then announce their title to the rest of the group, who must try to guess the author's name.

Here's an example: For cookbooks, one title might be *1,001 Salad Recipes*. The author: Leif E. Greens. Here's another title: *Mastering Outdoor Cooking* by Barbie Q. Sauce. Yet another: *Zen and the Art of Hot Covered Dishes* by Cass A. Role.
    Get the idea? The one must to this game is that the author's first name be real. Other than that, let your pun gland run amok. Another good idea is to keep your book categories fairly broad—history, sports, that sort of thing. This gives players the greatest leeway to think up the best titles. (Under the category "occupations," who was the author of *My Life as a Gas Station Attendant*? Phil A. Tank, naturally.)

❑ **How To Win:**   This is a tough game, since any book title presents a lot of punning possibilities. You may just want to play for the fun of it. However, if you're set on playing competitively, keep coming up with new titles until someone in the group guesses correctly. The winner is the player who stumps the others for the greatest number of turns.

◆

Bienvenue

This game of our own devising lets you—yes, you—think up those community welcoming slogans you see on billboards. However, our game also poses a little creative wrinkle.

❑ **Aim of the Game:** To use the letters in the name of a place to make up slogans that "welcome" you to the area.

❑ **Number of Players:** One or more.

❑ **Game Plan:** In multiplayer games, one participant provides another with the name of a place—it can be a city, state, country, or whatever, just so long as it's a place all the players know something about. The player whose turn it is must then think of the kind of phrase that you would see on a welcoming billboard. There are several rules—for one thing, the first word in the phrase must always be the name of the location. Additionally, the first letter of each word in the phrase must be the same as the letters in the name and must follow their order.

Here's an example: In tribute to Chicago's wondrous winters, one suitable slogan would be, "*C*hicago: *H*elping *I*cicles *C*ling *A*long *G*arage *O*verhangs." Makes you want to move there tomorrow, right? Here's another: For the college town of Eugene, Oregon, one fitting phrase would be, "*E*ugene: *U*nderstanding *G*raduates *E*xpect *N*ominal *E*mployment."

Don't limit yourself to cities: "*I*daho: *D*efinitely *A*ttractive, *H*ardly

Overpopulated." Don't even limit yourself to this world, if you like: "*Pluto: Looking Unusually Tiny Overhead.*"

Bienvenue can be played two ways. In one version, each player in the group has to come up with a slogan for a different place. A more challenging game requires all the players to make up slogans for the same place.

❑ **How To Win:** This game is fun enough on its own. But, if you've just got to compete, the player who comes up with the most creative or witty slogan can be named the winner.

❑ **Variation:** If you're traveling by car or train, one variation lets players take turns thinking up welcoming slogans as they pass through towns along the way. Rather than basing their phrases on prior knowledge, this game lets players cook up slogans based on what they see at the moment. Start the game at the outskirts of town, and give the player a couple of minutes to devise a slogan. This is also a good way to play the game solo.

Build Up

This game calls upon players to build a string of words that grows longer with every word. This is also a good solo game.

❑ **Aim of the Game:** To start and add to a series of ever-lengthening words, each of which contains all the letters from the previous word.

❑ **Number of Players:** One or more.

❏ **Game Plan:**   One player starts the game by naming a letter. The next player must then form a word by adding a second letter to the original one. The subsequent player must then form a three-letter word that includes the first two letters. Players need not keep the letters in the same order in which they were used by preceding players so long as they use all the letters. While it's okay to add a letter that's already part of the word, merely tacking on an *S* at the end to form a plural is not acceptable.

Here's how a game might go: The first player starts with the letter *A*. The next player says "at." The next player says "sat." The player after that could say something like "sate." The next player could shake things up a bit by suggesting "rates"—note how this uses all four of the prior letters but doesn't keep them in the same order.

   Play continues in this fashion, with players using the existing letters and adding a new one to form a new word. Subsequent turns in our example could have featured the words "baster," followed by "be-rates." The last word shows how a letter—in this case *E*—can be used more than once.

❏ **How To Win:**   Players drop out as they're unable to come up with a new word. The last player remaining is the winner.

❏ **Suggestions For Play:**   The player who starts the game must give the next player a letter that allows her to build a word. As such, letters such as *Q*, which have no two-letter possibilities, are not acceptable.

◆

Discipline

Here's an enjoyable game in which players are asked to imagine how some people get what's coming to them.

❑ **Aim of the Game:**   To devise a play on words around various occupations and how members of that occupation would be disciplined.

❑ **Number of Players:**   Two or more.

❑ **Game Plan:**   If military officers can be demoted, how are other occupations policed? With that idea in mind, players take turns devising a play on words that involves an occupation and its particular form of discipline. Example: One player could ask, "How would chimney builders be disciplined?" It's then up to the other players to come up with the answer: "They're dismantled." Other examples: A train conductor is derailed, an air conditioner installer is deducted, and a mentor is, understandably enough, demented.

Play may continue with players taking turns devising riddles, or one player can continue to make them up until another player guesses one. That player would then be charged with concocting the new riddle.

❑ **How To Win:**   This is one game where winners and losers are definitely a moot point. Just playing is fun and challenge enough.

❑ **Variation:**   If someone can be disciplined, they should also be given a second chance to make good. Accordingly, this game asks players to devise riddles about how certain occupations are reinstated. For instance, "How are battery makers reinstated?" "They're regenerated." Others include a sculptor (reformed), fashion industry workers (remodeled), and mathematicians (renumerated).

Ghost

A popular game that got to be that way by offering simple, yet challenging play that's easy to learn and entertaining, time and time again.

❑ **Aim of the Game:**   To add to a series of letters without forming a word.

❑ **Number of Players:**   Two or more.

❑ **Game Plan:**   One player starts the game by naming a letter. The next player adds a letter without forming a word but with a complete word in mind. Players take turns adding individual letters without making a word. A round of Ghost ends through one of two ways—one is when a player adds a letter that forms a word, thereby losing that round. The second involves a challenge from other players when they suspect that a player has added a letter without having a specific word in mind. The player who's challenged must then either reveal a word that can be formed from those letters or lose that round. Should a player successfully answer a challenge, the player who challenged loses that round.

Here's an example of how a round might go:
- **Player #1:**   M.
- **Player #2:**   M-U.
- **Player #3:**   M-U-L.
- **Player #4:**   M-U-L-B.
- **Player #1** challenges Player #4, who responds by announcing the word *mulberry*.

Once a round is finished, the next player in turn starts the next round by naming the first letter.

❑ **How To Win:**   Players who lose a round receive one letter in the word "Ghost"—once players accumulate "G-H-O-S-T," they're eliminated from the game. In a shorter version, the last player to successfully add a letter to the series is declared the winner of that particular round.

❑ **Variation:**   While the basic game only allows players to add letters to the end of a series, another version lets players add letters to either the front or the end of a series. In this version, as players add a letter, they should announce whether the letter goes at the beginning or the end of a series.

Here's an example:
- **Player #1:**   G.
- **Player #2:**   G-N.
- **Player #3:**   A-G-N.
- **Player #4:**   A-G-N-I.

- **Player #1:** A-G-N-I-F.
- **Player #2** challenges Player #1, who announces the word *magnificent*.

Guillotine

This alphabet-based game calls on the players' ability to think of words that could stand a little trim. Also good for solo play.

❏ **Aim of the Game:** To name words in an alphabetical order that, if the first letter is removed, still form a word.

❏ **Number of Players:** One or more.

❏ **Game Plan:** The first player starts by naming a word that begins with the letter *A*—the trick is to think of a word that also makes a word without the *A*. Example: The word "ahead" would be suitable since, without the letter *A*, the word "head" is formed. The next player must think of a similar word starting with *B*—"brain" would be good, since the word "rain" is formed by deleting the *B*. The next player takes the word starting with the letter *C*, and so on.

❏ **How To Win:** Players drop from the game as they're unable to come up with a suitable word.

❏ **Variations:** Players may agree to skip words beginning with *Q*, *X*, and *Z*, although those playing a competitive game may want to leave them in.

One variation of Guillotine requires all words used in a game to have the same number of letters.

An even more challenging version calls upon players to think of words in which the first *two* letters may be removed to form a new word. This game requires that the first of the two letters follow an alphabetical order, but the second letter can be anything. Here's an idea of how a game could start: "ascot" (cot), "balance" (lance), "clever" (ever). Combine this version with the rule stipulating word length for a really demanding game.

The Last Word

This wordplay game was invented by Dave Silverman. The Last Word first appeared in Word Ways *magazine.*

❑ **Aim of the Game:** To develop an alphabetical string of words that has one letter in common.

❑ **Number of Players:** Two or more.

❑ **Game Plan:** Players first agree on the length of the words for the game—for this example, let's say six. The first player names a six-letter word. The next player then names another six-letter word that would come after the first word in the dictionary. The second word must also have at least one "crash"—one letter that appears in the same position as in the first word. Play continues in this manner, with subsequent players naming words that share at least one "crash" letter with the prior word and which follow an alphabetical pattern.

Here's an example of a series of suitable words for a six-letter game:

- ● **Player #1:** Almost.
- ● **Player #2:** Become.
- ● **Player #3:** Demand.
- ● **Player #4:** Famous.
- ● **Player #1:** Gallop.

Note that the crash letter can change constantly—in the first and second word, it was the letter *O*, followed by *E* in the second and third word.

❑ **How To Win:** Winners can be determined in two ways. Play can continue once through the alphabet, and the player who names the last word wins. Players can also view the game circularly, with the letter *A* following the letter *Z*. In this version, players drop from the game as they're unable to think of a word that continues the series. The last player remaining is the winner.

❑ **Variation:** For an even more challenging version of the Last Word, players can be required to come up with two crash letters in each word.

List Switch

This starts out as your basic build-an-alphabetical-list game. Our version lets players strategically switch categories along the way.

❑ **Aim of the Game:** To build an alphabetical list within a predetermined category.

❑ **Number of Players:**   Two or more.

❑ **Game Plan:**   The first player starts by choosing a category for the game. This player then names something that begins with the letter *A* that fits the category. The next player must then name something that starts with the letter *B* that also fits the category. Play continues this way through the alphabet.

The wrinkle is that players, at their own discretion, may change the category of the game by naming a word that works in the current category but suggests another one. Here's an example: Let's say the game starts with movies as the category. The first player starts by saying "Amadeus." The next player says "Bang the Drum Slowly." The next player says "Camelot." The following player says "Damn Yankees" and adds that he's switching the category to sports teams names. The next player must then come up with a team name beginning with *E:* "Emeralds" (yup, that's the name of a baseball team in Eugene, Oregon).

The next player then must come up with a team beginning with *F*: she says "Forty Niners," which the next player follows with "Giants." The following player says "Hornets" and announces that she's switching the category to things that fly. That forces the next player to name something that flies that starts with the letter *I*, such as "insects."

Another wrinkle is that any player who announces a category switch must have a word in mind that fits the new category as well as that particular alphabetical position. The next player in line may choose to challenge the player who switched the category—the challenged player must then name a word that fits the new category. If she can do so, the challenging player is eliminated; if the challenged player switches the category without having a new word that fits, she is eliminated.

This example gives you a good idea of how the game works. For one thing, you don't have to change the category, even though you've got a word that would allow you to do it. Rather, in a competitive game, category switching works best by moving play into an area where it will be difficult for the next player to come up with a correct answer—provided, of course, that you've got a word in mind that fits the new category.

❑ **How to Win:**   Players are eliminated as they're unable to come up with a word that fits the category. The last player remaining is the winner.

❑ **Suggestions For Play:**   It's a good idea to keep categories fairly broad so players can compete fairly. During the course of a game players may reject by consensus a category suggestion if they think it's too narrow.

There are two schools of thought about keeping the letters X and Z in a game. On the one hand, some players might wish to eliminate them, as they offer little in the way of possibilities. On the other hand, other players may think X and Z are important parts of a competitive game—if you happen to get them, that's the luck of the draw.

◆

The Oxydental Tourist

This tests your ability to remember or create oxymorons—pairs of words that contradict one another. Like other games that involve wordplay, this one can occasionally get pretty ugly. Get it?

❏ **Aim of the Game:** Players list oxymorons in an alphabetical order.

❏ **Number of Players:** One or more.

❏ **Game Plan:** The first player starts by thinking of an oxymoron whose first word begins with the letter *A*. It can be a well-known oxymoron or one the player has thought up himself. One possibility would be "amicable divorce." Or how about "amorphous shape"? Once he has his oxymoron in mind, the player announces it to the other players.

The next player is then charged with coming up with a *B* oxymoron, such as "bad health." The following player then continues with a *C* oxymoron. If you read a lot of popular fiction, then "creative writing" might be a suitable contradiction in terms. There's even one for those who doubt the value of higher schooling: "college education."
  Play continues through the alphabet.

❏ **How To Win:** Players drop from the game as they're unable to suggest a suitable oxymoron. The last player left is the winner.

❏ **Suggestions For Play:** This can be a tough game, so players should be allowed at least a couple of minutes to come up with a suggestion that fits a particular letter. Players should also give each other a fair amount of creative leeway. When someone announces an oxymoron you haven't heard of before, take a moment and consider whether the expression strikes a good contradiction in terms. However, if someone comes up with a rather lame suggestion, the other players can make him think up another oxymoron or drop him from that particular game.

Possession

Just can't seem to let go sometimes? This might be the game you've been holding out for.

❏ **Aim of the Game:** To think up names that can be used as a form of possession.

❏ **Number of Players:** One version requires at least two players; the second may be played solo.

❏ **Game Plan:** In the two-player version of Possession, one player starts by thinking of a person's name that, taking the two words, can be transformed into a possessive. Here are some examples: George Bush (George's Bush), Jimmy Buffett (Jimmy's Buffett), and Barney Fife (Barney's Fife).

From there, the player must devise a clue to offer to the other players—the clue, however vaguely, must suggest the Possession. For instance, using George's Bush, one suitable clue might be "Former president's shrubbery." For Jimmy's Buffett, a good clue would be "A musician's turbulence." In the Barney Fife example, one possibility would be "A musical instrument belonging to Andy Griffith's side-kick."

In the two-player version of Possession, players may take turns thinking up names and offering clues. When more than two are playing, the person who guesses the last Possession must come up with the next name and appropriate clue.

❑ **How To Win:** Players must try to stump the other players by coming up with particularly tricky Possessions and/or clues.

❑ **Variation:** One twist to Possession calls upon players to think up possessions in alphabetical order. For instance, the first player would have to come up with a Possession whose last name begins with the letter *A*: "Neil's Armstrong" (a powerful appendage attached to an astronaut). The next player would then be charged with thinking up a *B* Possession—in this case, how about "Warren's Burger" (a former Supreme Court justice's lunch). This version allows for solo play.

◆

Tom Swifties

This is a game that's been played for years—and with good reason. It requires quick thinking, wit, and the gift for wordplay to notice things others might miss.

❑ **Aim of the Game:**   To devise thematic sentences using a punning adverb.

❑ **Number of Players:**   Two or more.

❑ **Game Plan:**   Players choose a category to follow—let's say the theme is the presidency. The first player must come up with a Tom Swifty around this idea. Here's one: "The president will use his veto," he said haltingly. This Tom Swifty shows how the adverb at the end of the sentence puns the meaning of what's been said. The next player may add something like this: "It's too bad his election was rigged," he said stuffily. Yet another: "Will he run for re-election?" he asked repeatedly.

Play continues as players build Tom Swifties around the theme.

❑ **How To Win:**   In a competitive game, the winner is the last player who's able to come up with a Tom Swifty within the confines of a category.

◆

Veg Out

This wordplay game suggested by the Ludlow family of Wilsonville, Oregon, is the only one in this book that helps meet your minimum daily requirement for roughage.

❏ **Aim of the Game:**   Players devise sentences in which the name of a vegetable is hidden.

❏ **Number of Players:**   Two or more.

❏ **Game Plan:**   One player thinks of a sentence in which the name of a vegetable is hidden. That can take several forms—while the name of the vegetable can appear in its literal form, the best ones group syllables from separate words in a phonetic combination. The remaining players then try to guess the name of the vegetable.

Here are some examples to get you started:
> *Sue held out her plate, remarking, "This casserole is rad, dish me up some more." (radish)*
> *When Jewish people have a question about their faith, they call a rabbi. (kohlrabi)*
> *He told the guru, "Barbed wire is sharp." (rhubarb)*

Players take turns devising sentences and guessing.

❏ **How To Win:**   While you can try to stump the other players, this kind of wordplay is a great deal of fun without the competition.

❑ **Variation:** Veg Out also works with fruits instead of vegetables. Here are a couple of ideas:

Bill grew angry and shouted, "You sap, pull on the rope harder!" (apple)

The doctor told the couple, "To mate over and over again is tiring." (tomato)

There's an old saying: To be happy, choose your friends carefully. (peaches)

Word Series

This game, invented by Doug and Jan Heller, tests your ability to make something out of nothing.

❑ **Aim of the Game:** To discern a word based on only a few letters from the word.

❑ **Number of Players:** Two or more.

❑ **Game Plan:** One player thinks of a word—the longer the word, the more interesting the game. The player then selects three letters that are located in sequence within the word and announces them to the remaining players.

The next player then tries to guess the word based on the three letters she's been given. If she can't, the first player adds another letter, building on either at the beginning or the end of the letters already given. The next player then tries to guess the word—if she's incorrect, the first player adds yet another letter, and so on, until one of the other players guesses the word.

Here's how a three-player game might go. The first player thinks of the word "diversionary" and announces the letters E-R-S to the other two players:

- **Player #2:** Is the word superstitious?
- **Player #1:** No. V-E-R-S.
- **Player #3:** Is the word diversify?
- **Player #1:** No. V-E-R-S-I.
- **Player #2:** Is the word version?
- **Player #1:** No. I-V-E-R-S-I.
- **Player #3:** Is the word university?
- **Player #1:** No. I-V-E-R-S-I-O.
- **Player #2:** Is the word diversion?
- **Player #1:** No. I-V-E-R-S-I-O-N.
- **Player #3:** Is the word diversionary?

❑ **How To Win:**   Players take turns thinking up words and trying to stump the others. The player whose word requires the greatest number of guesses is the winner.

❑ **Suggestions For Play:**   You'll note in the above example that the word diversionary was an offshoot from the more common word diversion. This makes play more challenging—it was only by getting past the word diversion that Player #3 realized that the mystery had to be some variation on that word.

◆

Word Tag

This is a simple game of word association. The object can either be to stump your opponent or to keep the string going as long as possible.

❑ **Aim of the Game:** To take a word used by another player and use it in a well-known phrase, name, or title.

❑ **Number of Players:** Two or more.

❑ **Game Plan:** Here's an example of how a game might go. Player #1 starts the game by announcing a word—in this case, the player says "go." Player #2 then uses that word to create "Go Fish." A good answer for Player #3 would be something like "A fish out of water."

In Word Tag, no word may be used by more than two players in a row. As such, note that in the above example, Player #3 didn't use the word "go," since it was used by the first two players. As a result, Player #4 would be charged with coming up with a phrase using either "water" or "out," since the word "fish" was used twice and therefore eliminated. Words may be reintroduced once players are past the point where the word has been used twice in a row.

Articles and prepositions cannot be used as part of Word Tag. Should a player offer a phrase that contains a large number of words, the subsequent player has his choice of which word he wants to use in a phrase. As an example, should the next player in the preceding example say "Water, water everywhere, but not a drop to drink," the next player could choose from "everywhere," "drop," and "drink" (following the rule that eliminates the word "water" from further play).

Players are eliminated when they cannot think of a phrase to keep the string alive.

❏ **How To Win:** The last player who's still in the game is declared the winner.

❏ **Variation:** Try playing with a time limit—a time crunch can often result in some amusing answers.

Yuppie Puppy

A new name for an old standard. This is an ideal travel game, since the only required equipment is a general sense of what might rhyme with what, as well as a generous shot of creativity.

❏ **Aim of the Game:** To describe a person, place, event, or action with a two-word rhyme.

❏ **Number of Players:** Two or more.

❏ **Game Plan:** Players agree on turns, and the first offers a clue that suggests a two-word rhyme as its answer. Example: Using the nifty new title we've come up with, one player might suggest the clue, "a young, urban, upwardly mobile dog," to which the correct response would be "Yuppie Puppy."

Other Yuppie Puppies to get you started include "jiggling television evangelist" (Shaker Bakker), "overweight domestic automobile" (Heavy Chevy), and "nebulous poultry" (murky turkey).

❑ **How To Win:** Players may be eliminated from further play as they miss Yuppie Puppies—the last one to correctly identify one may be declared the winner. This, however, is a game in which no competition is necessary—devising clever Yuppie Puppies and offering them to another player or a group is great fun in and of itself.

❑ **Variations:** There are also such things as Yup Pups, Yuppie Pups, and Yup Puppies. The first type is when the first and second words of the answer both contain one syllable—for instance, "an outrageously wealthy man's garbage heap" (Trump Dump) is a Yup Pup. An example of a Yuppie Pup is "a late-hour airplane ride" (midnight flight), while a Yup Puppy might be "angry Middle Eastern city" (mad Baghdad).

Some players think it's important that answers contain the same number of syllables—before your game starts, decide if that's necessary or not. If you like, as you give the clue, you may tell the other players if it's a Yuppie Puppy or one of the others.

In another version called "Uppity Yuppie Puppy," the game is extended an additional word—as such, all answers contain three words. While the name of this game may be the correct answer to a clue such as "a highbrow, upwardly mobile young dog," other examples include "someone who's gone beyond an unfortunate social trend" (bad fad grad), and "anxiety caused by proximity to an alcoholic beverage" (near beer fear).

Mystery and Guessing Games

"*Mystery is the wisdom of blockheads.*"

—Horace Walpole

Botticelli

Botticelli is an old-line party game that is well-suited to travel. For all its notoriety, however, the origin of the game's name remains one of life's eternal, cryptic riddles, like Stonehenge or the mercifully short-lived popularity of disco.

❑ **Aim of the Game:**   To guess a mystery name by asking a series of questions.

❑ **Number of Players:**   Two or more.

❑ **Game Plan:**   This game is best explained by example. Let's say Player #1 has thought of Scott Fitzgerald as the mystery name—so he tells the other players that the initials for the game are "SF." From there, player #2, thinking that the person might be Sigmund Freud, could ask, "Are you considered the father of modern psychology?" If Player #1 knows the person the question suggests, he can answer, "No, I am not Sigmund Freud," and play continues to Player #3. If she thinks the mystery person might be actress Sally Field, she could ask, "Did you once play the Flying Nun?" If Player #1 knows whom that refers to, he could respond, "No, I am not Sally Field," and play would go on.

Should the player with the mystery not know the person to whom a question refers or if he answers incorrectly, the player who asked the question may ask a second question that has a yes or no answer. For instance, if a player asked, "Are you a cartoon character who's also a working mother?" (referring to the "Sally Forth" comic strip) and Player #1 did not answer correctly, the player who posed the question could then ask something like, "Are you female?" "Are you a fictional character?" or "Are you living?" These kinds of questions help the guessing players obtain important details about the mystery.

❑ **How To Win:** Play continues until the players either give up or one poses a question that identifies the mystery person. In this example, that could be, "Did you write *The Great Gatsby*?"

❑ **Suggestions For Play:** In choosing names for Botticelli, players should agree to use only very well-known people—as you can see, it can be tough trying to think of names that match the given initials. In addition, most people prefer to play this game using only two-initial names. With apologies to everyone from Charo to Joyce Carol Oates, one-letter and three-letter initials are usually either too hard or too easy.

Clued In

This is an engaging guessing game that features initial-based clues.

❑ **Aim of the Game:** To guess a famous person's name using a two-word clue. The first letters of the two words must be the same as the initials of the mystery person's name.

❏ **Number of Players:** Two or more.

❏ **Game Plan:** One player thinks of a well-known person, then gives the other players a two-word hint. The wrinkle is that the first two letters of the hint should be the same as the mystery person's initials. Players must then try to guess the mystery person.

Example: One hint might be "Battling Congress"—that would work with Bill Clinton. The clue "Superstar Orlando" would certainly go with Shaquille O'Neal. And the clue "Daily Latenight" could only suggest David Letterman.

❏ **How To Win:** Players can try to stump one another with their clues, but this is yet another game where play can be entertaining enough without any sort of competition.

The challenge of this game comes at both ends. While it can be difficult to guess the mystery person, coming up with clever clues that also match a person's initials can be tough. It takes some thought to devise an effective clue within the constraint of those two letters.

❏ **Variation:** A more difficult version of Clued In lets the player who made up the mystery offer additional clues if the other players can't guess the mystery from the initial two-word hint. The challenge is that any additional clues, like the first one, must follow the same pattern of initials. For instance, in the Bill Clinton example listed above, another suitable clue might be "Badly Coiffed." Another clue from the Shaquille O'Neal example could be "Salary Outrageous." The players should be given a chance to guess the mystery after each additional clue.

Coffeepot

A favorite guessing game, great for young and old alike.

❏ **Aim of the Game:**   To guess a mystery action using questions with a yes or no answer.

❏ **Number of Players:**   Two or more.

❏ **Game Plan:**   One player thinks of an action. The remaining players then ask closed-ended questions, substituting the word, "coffeepot" when they refer to the mystery. The player with the mystery answers yes or no, and players use this information to determine the mystery.

Say one player thinks of swimming as the mystery action. The next player might ask, "Can you coffeepot at night?" to which the first player would say yes. The next player might then ask, "Can everyone coffeepot?" and the first player would say no. And so on, until one player guesses the mystery.

❏ **Suggestions for Play:**   The idea behind Coffeepot is to proceed logically to more narrowly focused questions. The more general your questions are, the longer the mystery will remain.

❏ **Variations:** The basic format calls for players to take turns answering questions, regardless of the answer. One twist that can sharpen the competitiveness of the game is for a player to keep asking questions so long as he or she is getting a yes answer. That also helps a player follow through on a particular idea.

Dig It, Man

Shades of Maynard G. Krebs—this game tests players' abilities to dig the "man" hidden within words.

❏ **Aim of the Game:** To devise mystery questions whose answers contain the word "man."

❏ **Number of Players:** Two or more.

❏ **Game Plan:** Players think of cryptic questions whose one-word answers contain the word "man." The remaining players have to come up with the correct answer.

For instance, "Where's the man in New York City?" would result in the answer "Manhattan." Likewise, the query "Where's the man in China?" would be properly answered by "Manchuria."

The questions don't have to address geography. Try this one: "Where's the man in a large company?" Answer: "Management." Nor does *man* have to come at the beginning of the answer: "Where's the man in a famous Native American tribe?" Answer: "Comanche."

❑ **How To Win:** Players can try to stump the rest of the group, but this game is perfectly entertaining without an element of competition.

❑ **Variation:** For those less than enamored with the idea of pursuing our little friend, try Dig That Cat. The idea here is identical, only the word cat is the mystery element that has to be uncovered. Here are a couple to get you started: "Where's the cat in Spain?" Answer: "Catalonia." Here's a tough one: "Where's the cat mentioned in an Asian city in a Bob Seger song?" Reply: "Katmandu." This example shows that the answer doesn't have to be spelled exactly the same as "cat," but only match it phonetically.

Freudian Trip

This game, suggested by our buddy Jeff Wallach, is particularly good for outings where you might be spending time with people about whom you know very little. While often outrageously funny, the game also encourages players to share some revealing facts about themselves.

❑ **Aim of the Game:** To say three things about yourself and fool the other players as to which of the three statements is false.

❑ **Number of Players:** Two or more. The more, the better.

❑ **Game Plan:** One player starts the game by saying three things about himself—two of the statements are true, one is not. In turn, the remaining players guess which statement they think is not the truth.

For every one that guesses incorrectly, the player receives one point. Play then switches to another player, who offers the group three statements about himself—the group then tries to identify which statement is not the truth about that player.

Here's an example that one of us offered recently. The answer is provided at the end of this game:

1. A large article—complete with a photograph—was once written about me in *The Asbury Park Press*.
2. I once danced with Gene Hackman's daughter at a high-school dance.
3. I was the starting tight end on my high-school football team.

❑ **How To Win:** Although this game is great fun unto itself, the player who fools the most players at the end of each round may be declared the winner.

❑ **Variations:** Players may choose to write down their guesses rather than announcing them out loud. This often provides a greater variety of answers, since it eliminates the possibility of simply agreeing with another player's opinion.

Another variation calls upon players to offer three statements, but in this version players must say two that are lies and one that's the truth. The other players must then decide which of the three statements is true.

Yet another twist calls upon the guessing players to reach a consensus rather than having each player offer individual guesses. Since this version promotes group discussion about the player who made the three statements, this version of Freudian Trip can be particularly eye-opening, as players share their thoughts and opinions about other players.

Solution: The third statement about my playing tight end is false. I've long since lost the press clipping which dealt with my participation in a college honors program—the picture was silly, anyway. And, for all you tinsel-town tattler types, Gene Hackman's daughter was very nice. I trust she still is.

Hackensack Hatchback

This is one of the best adult travel games we've come across. By the way, if you don't care for the name, feel free to devise an alliterative title of your own—Tallahassee Trunk, Utica U-Haul, Wenatchee Winnebago, whatever.

❑ **Aim of the Game:** To guess a secret category of words devised by one of the players.

❑ **Number of Players:** Two or more.

❑ **Game Plan:** One of the players thinks of a secret category of words and offers a clue that hints at the category. The clue is always given in the form of the phrase: "My hatchback is packed and I'm headed for Hackensack. I'm packing————," at which point the player tells the others one of the things he is taking. The item, however subtly, must fit the secret category.

Example: The player giving the clues is thinking of items that require batteries. This player says, "My hatchback is packed and I'm headed for Hackensack. I'm packing my flashlight." Another player might ask, "I'd like to pack a candle. Can I come, too?" The player with the secret category must answer no and offer another clue, which could take the following form: "No, you may not come, but I'm also packing my hearing aid." Play continues with questions and additional clues until one or all of the players suggest an item that fits the secret category. One instance of a player guessing correctly could be, "If I pack my portable radio, can I come, too?" at which the lead player tells that player yes, he may head for Hackensack. Notice that the actual category isn't identified, only that the player has offered a suitable suggestion.

❑ **How To Win:**   The winner of the game may be the first player to correctly identify something that fits the mystery category. That player may then take a turn thinking up another mystery category and offering clues. The game may also continue until all the players have offered acceptable suggestions.

Another variation requires a player to correctly identify the category once that player has named something that fits. This version eliminates inadvertently correct answers.

❑ **Suggestions for Play:**   In devising categories, players can be as broad or as specific as they feel is reasonable. Categories such as words beginning with a particular letter, items located within a car, and words having to do with the novel *Moby Dick* are all examples of good choices.

❑ **Variations:** One variation is Paradoxical Hackensack Hatchback. In this game, the player with the mystery category mentions two contradictory clues—the clues seem to make no sense at first, but they both hint at the mystery category. For example, to use the instance cited above, the player giving the clues may have started with, "My hatchback is packed and I'm headed for Hackensack. I'm packing my flashlight but not a flaming torch." Similarly, with the second clue given he might have said "I'm packing my hearing aid, but not an old-fashioned hearing trumpet."

Another version is Personality Hackensack Hatchback, in which all the clues given by the player with the mystery suggest a well-known person. For instance, if the mystery person is actor Dustin Hoffman, one way to start the game would be to say, "My hatchback is packed and I'm headed for Hackensack. I'm packing Anne Bancroft." Another suggestion would be, "I'm packing a Tootsie Roll." As such, any player who said she was packing her "graduate degree" or "reporter's note-book" (referring to *All the President's Men*) would be allowed to come along. With this version, it's important to suggest people who not only are well known but who also suggest associated clues that will be readily recognized by the other players.

Another twist is Historical Hackensack Hatchback, in which famous events are used. Where would you be heading if you packed a golf club, a flag, and a custom dune buggy? (The moon landing, that's where.)

You may wish to keep different versions of Hackensack Hatchback separate by identifying beforehand which one you're playing. The game takes on an added challenge, however, when the clues you're giving may apply to any version.

Interior Design

This is an imaginative question-and-answer game where players try to identify a mystery person by asking questions that address that person's inner qualities. Hence our clever name.

❑ **Aim of the Game:**   To identify a real or fictional person.

❑ **Number of Players:**   Two or more.

❑ **Game Plan:**   One player thinks of a person and tells the remaining players whether the character is real or fictional. In turn, the other players ask questions whose answers compare that person with something else. The comparison should suggest something about that mystery person's character and help the guessing players identify the mystery.

Here's a sample: One player thinks of Winston Churchill and tells the remaining players that the mystery person is real. The game might then proceed along these lines, with players taking turns asking questions:

- **Question:**   What kind of book would this person be?
- **Answer:**   Serious history.
- **Question:**   What kind of music would this person be?
- **Answer:**   A bold, defiant symphony.
- **Question:**   What kind of building would this person be?
- **Answer:**   A solid brick building built low to the ground.
- **Question:**   What kind of animal would this person be?
- **Answer:**   Definitely a bulldog.

Notice how the answers actually offer two types of clues. While certain aspects of the answers hint at Churchill's character—defiant, bold, serious—references to history and bulldogs offer direct suggestions about his nationality and interests.

Notice, too, that the player with the mystery has a good deal of creative license when devising her answers. She can make some replies fairly straightforward, while others can be a good deal more cryptic. However, all her answers should offer some insight or information into the personality—and identity—of the mystery character.

Players' questions may deal with any topic—restaurants, automobiles, clothing, the weather, you name it—anything that may elicit an answer that's particularly suggestive or indicative of the mystery person.

When a player's turn comes he may try to guess the identity of the mystery person prior to asking a question. Should a player guess incorrectly, he is not allowed to ask a question during that turn, and play moves on to the next player.

❏ **How To Win:** A round continues until one player guesses the mystery or the players give up. If you want to compete, the player whose mystery requires the greatest number of questions to solve can be declared the winner.

❏ **Variation:** For a particularly provocative game, try making one of the players in the group the mystery person—that's sure to make for interesting play.

Kolodny's Game

This game, invented by David Greene Kolodny, is one of the most demanding we've ever come across. It's a good choice if players are looking for a challenging game that's likely to last a while. If you're interested in something a bit more quick and dirty, you might want to look elsewhere.

❑ **Aim of the Game:** To determine the rule of the game by asking yes or no questions.

❑ **Number of Players:** Two or more.

❑ **Game Plan:** One player devises the "rule" for the game. In Kolodny's Game, that rule determines which questions require a yes answer and which questions require a no. This means that the answers are dictated by the *content* of the question rather than the question itself.

Let's say one player decides that the rule of the game is that all questions that contain the words *a* or *an* require a yes answer—all others call for a no reply. The remaining players then take turns asking yes or no questions to uncover the rule.
   Here's how a game might start off:
   ● **Question:** Is this a word game?   YES.
   ● **Question:** Is the game difficult?   NO.
   ● **Question:** Is the game particularly easy?   NO.
   ● **Question:** Does the game deal with a number?   YES.
   ● **Question:** You mean it's numerical?   NO.

You'll see that the answers don't really "answer" the question, nor do the questions necessarily have to have any sort of relationship with one another. Rather, players should look for patterns and other recurring clues that suggest a common feature about all questions that require a yes answer.

Players may guess when they think they've discovered the rule. Incorrect guesses count as a turn, and play moves on to the next player.

❏ **How To Win:**   The player who uncovers the rule is the winner and may, if he wishes, think up a new rule for a new game.

❏ **Suggestions for Play:**   Try to keep rules fairly broad so that players have a reasonable chance of figuring them out. As such, a rule that says all questions four words or longer require a yes answer, three words or shorter require a no would be an example of a good, workable rule. On the other hand, overly picayune rules—the fourth letter of the second word has to be a vowel to get a yes answer—make the game unplayable.

◆

Letter Logic

This game calls upon players' command of logic as they figure out a mystery word.

❑ **Aim of the Game:** To guess a mystery word using process of elimination.

❑ **Number of Players:** Two or more.

❑ **Game Plan:** Players agree on the number of letters in the mystery word. One player thinks of the word and another player starts the game by naming a word containing the same number of letters. If any of the letters in that word match those in the mystery word and are also in the same spot, the player with the mystery word tells the other player how many letters are correct and in the proper position.

Example: Let's say a game starts with *bit* as the mystery word, and the guessing player begins with the word *tab*. The first player announces "zero," since, even though the word contains two correct letters, they're not in the correct position. The guessing player then says *cat*, to which the other player says "one," since the *T* is correct and in the right spot. The guessing player then suggests *cut*, the idea being to narrow down which of the three letters is correct—when "one" is announced, the player knows it's either the *C* or the *T*. Luckily, the player then says *but*, for which the correct answer is "two." From there, the player should have little trouble in eventually coming to the word *bit*.

❏ **How To Win:**   Players count the number of turns it takes to figure out the mystery and the game continues with a different player thinking of a new mystery word. The player who requires the least number of turns to decipher the mystery word is the winner. Make certain that all the words contain the same number of letters.

❏ **Variations:**   One variant of Letter Logic requires the player with the mystery to let other players know about correct letters that are not in the correct position. For instance, in the example above, the correct response to the first suggestion of *tab* would have been "two," since two letters are correct, even though they're not in the right spots. This version can either make the game easier or more challenging, since the knowledge that certain letters are correct is offset by uncertainty as to their correct position.

In games in which more than two people are playing, one player devises the mystery word while the others take turns offering guesses. In this version, the winner is the player whose word takes the greatest number of turns to decipher.

Story Line

This game offers a two-way challenge—not only are players called on to guess a mystery title, but one player must also devise a clever story to describe the secret.

❏ **Aim of the Game:**   Players must guess a mystery title based on clues from a story invented by another player.

❑ **Number of Players:** Two or more.

❑ **Game Plan:** One player is chosen to think up the mystery title—it can be a book, television program, movie, song title, or anything else with a well-known title. From there, the player thinks up a brief story that cryptically describes the title without clearly identifying it. The player then announces the title's category—book, TV show, whatever—and tells his story to the remaining players, who must guess the title. If asked, the player who devised the story must repeat it so the remaining players can hear it more than once, but the guessing players may not ask any additional questions about the story.

Here's one: One player thinks of the book *From Here To Eternity*, informs the other players that he has a book title in mind, then tells the following story. "One day I was driving toward a large city—you might have heard of it, its twin city is Infinity. Anyway, I got lost, so I stopped a cop along the road to ask for directions. He gave them to me, but he wasn't sure how far away the city was. 'I know how far it is to Infinity, but the other one has me stumped,' the cop confessed. 'Well,' I replied, 'I'd really like to know how far it is _____.' "

As you can tell from the preceding example, players should offer clues that give the other players enough information with which to solve the riddle, only not so many that it becomes too obvious. Synonyms, plays on words, and puns are good elements to consider when devising a mystery—for instance, a player could describe the book *Bourne Identity* along the lines of a brand-new baby's personality.

❑ **How To Win:** Who cares? Making up challenging stories and trying to guess them is fun enough.

Tonto

Enjoy the lowest form of humor? If so, this guessing game invented by Pat McCormick will undoubtedly be right up your alley. Like other games in this collection, it's entirely verbal, so there's no need for the write stuff. Ahem.

❑ **Aim of the Game:**   To answer a question about a well-known person with a punned answer.

❑ **Number of Players:**   Two or more.

❑ **Game Plan:**   One player thinks of a question that describes a famous person. In responding, another player must begin the answer with "No" and use the person's name as a pun to answer the question correctly.

Example: An appropriate question might be, "Is the composer of the 'Hallelujah Chorus' a lock on a suitcase?" In turn, the correct response would be, "No, Joseph Handel." Other examples include: "Should the evangelist's wife broil her own mother?" "No, Tammy Faye Bakker"; and "Is a former president a primitive weapon?", "No, Ronald Reagan."

❑ **How To Win:**   One way to play Tonto is to have a player keep answering questions until he misses. The number answered correctly is totaled, and the player amassing the greatest number wins. If you're not interested in competing and would rather just wallow in wit, you can simply alternate who's asking and answering the questions.

❑ **Variations:** To make devising questions more of a challenge, games can be broken down into categories of particular subjects: politicians, writers, actors, and sports figures are just a few suggestions.

Twenty Questions

Okay, most everybody knows how to play Twenty Questions, and with good reason—challenging and entertaining, it's been one of the most popular games for a number of years. However, we've included a basic rundown of this most enjoyable adult travel game for those who need a quick review.

❑ **Aim of the Game:** To guess a secret using a series of questions that can be answered yes or no. The secret must be uncovered in twenty questions or less.

❑ **Number of Players:** Two or more.

❑ **Game Plan:** One player thinks of a person (real or fictional), place, or thing. The remaining players then take turns asking that player questions that can be answered with either a yes or no response. Players attempt to solve the mystery by process of identification and elimination.

Here's a sample sequence: One player thinks of the secret—in this case, let's say ice hockey great Gordie Howe. The sequence of questions and answers might proceed as follows:

- **1.** Is it an animal?   NO.
- **2.** Is it fictional?   NO.
- **3.** Is it human?   YES.
- **4.** Is it living?   YES.
- **5.** Is it an American?   No.
- **6.** Is it a North American?   YES.
- **7.** Is it widely known?   YES.
- **8.** Is it female?   No.
- **9.** Did he have anything to do with politics?   NO.
- **10.** Did he have anything to do with the arts?   NO.
- **11.** Did he have anything to do with sports?   YES.
- **12.** Was it a sport played in the winter?   YES.
- **13.** Did he play basketball?   NO.
- **14.** Did he play ice hockey?   YES.
- **15.** Did he play for Chicago?   NO.
- **16.** Did he play for Detroit?   YES.
- **17.** Was he a prolific goal scorer?   YES.
- **18.** Is it Gordie Howe?   YES.

Once you've established that the subject is human, getting past the question of real or fictional narrows the possibilities considerably. As such, the general idea is to construct an orderly sequence of questions that narrows the possibilities as efficiently as possible.

❏ **How To Win:** The guessing players win if they guess the secret in twenty questions or less. The player with the secret wins if the other players fail to identify the secret in twenty questions. An incorrect guess counts as a question.

❏ **Suggestions For Play:** The person who devises the secret should have a fairly extensive knowledge of the subject to ensure accurate answers.

Word to the Wise

Well-known sayings, slogans, proverbs, and even clichés are the focus of this question-and-answer game.

❏ **Aim of the Game:** Players attempt to identify a proverb by asking questions.

❏ **Number of Players:** Two or more.

❏ **Game Plan:** One player thinks of a well-known saying, proverb, or slogan, then tells the guessing players into which of those general categories the mystery falls. The remaining players take turns asking questions that require something other than a yes or no answer. When responding to the first question the player with the mystery must somehow include the first word from the saying. He must follow this system in subsequent answers, including the second word of the saying in his answer to the second question, and so on, until the guessing players are able to piece the pertinent words together and identify the slogan.

For instance, one player thinks of the expression, "You can lead a horse to water, but you can't make him drink." He then tells the other players that he has a proverb in mind. A game might follow these lines:

- **Player #1:** How are things going today?
- **Answer:** *You* can tell things are fine.
- **Player #2:** What are your plans for dinner tonight?
- **Answer:** Just a *can* of soup, I guess.
- **Player #3:** How's school been?
- **Answer:** Sometimes I feel like they *lead* me around by the nose.
- **Player #1:** Any vacation plans yet?
- **Answer:** *A* trip to the coast, I imagine.
- **Player #2:** Bringing the kids with you?
- **Answer:** No, they *horse* around too much.

Notice that the questions can really be about anything. Notice, too, that the answers make the game seem like a fairly normal conversation, even though the mystery slogan is hidden in the answers.

Play continues until either the guessing players identify the mystery or the player with the mystery gives clues for all the words in the mystery. If someone guesses the mystery, that player then devises a new mystery for the next round of play. If no one comes up with the mystery, then the player who devised that mystery thinks up a new one.

❏ **How To Win:** It's fun enough to play Word to the Wise without keeping score. However, if you want to compete, award a point every time a player guesses a mystery or a player stumps the others with a mystery. The first player to get five points (or any other number you like) wins the game.

❑ **Variations:** As noted above, you can use a whole array of proverbs, wise old sayings, advertising slogans, and even clichés (for a real challenge, try something like, "So, do you come here often?" provided, of course, that your stomach can take it.) Just make sure to clearly identify the category the mystery belongs to so the guessing players have some sort of focus.

License Plate and Travel Sign Games

"We Americans pretend 55 is the speed limit, similar to the way we're always pretending we want people to have a nice day, but it clearly isn't the real speed limit, since nobody, including the police, actually drives that slowly, except people wearing hats in the left lane."

—Dave Barry

Another Roadside Deduction

This game is particularly good if you're traveling on a highway with a large number of road signs.

❑ **Aim of the Game:** To use names—or parts of names—in a variety of phrases, titles, or in other recognizable ways.

❑ **Number of Players:** One or more.

❑ **Game Plan:** In turn, each player chooses a name on a highway sign. He must then take the name—or any portion of it—and use it in three different, recognizable ways, such as titles, common expressions, and well-known phrases. As an example, in passing a sign that says "Portland," a player may come up with sayings such as, "Any *port* in a storm," "It's an either *or* situation," and 'This *land* is your land."

Players may not use the identical portion of a word more than once —for instance, in the Portland example described above, it's okay to use "port" and "or," but a player saying "Any port in a storm" and "port of call" in the same turn would have to come up with something else.

The next player waits for a sign with a different name on it and play continues.

Since this is a spoken game, it's okay to take some liberties—thus, when you see a name like "Seattle," a suggestion such as "See Jane Run" is acceptable. Moreover, plays on words, puns, and other liberties should also be encouraged—as such, when using the name "Tacoma," "There's no place like oma" or "Ta Err is Human" must, in a tolerant society such as ours, be accepted.

Players are eliminated if they cannot come up with three suitable suggestions from a roadside name.

❑ **How To Win:**   The last player to successfully name three suggestions from a roadside sign is the winner.

❑ **Variations:**   To make the game either easier or more difficult, you can reduce or increase the number of suggestions a player must devise. See how it goes and arrive at a number that's comfortable. Also, rather than having the player choose her own word from a sign, a more challenging version has someone else do the choosing. This inevitably results in a more difficult word, particularly with signs that have several names from which to choose.

Creative License

This game lets players use license plates in a test of their literary skills.

❑ **Aim of the Game:**   To use license plate letters to create a story.

❑ **Number of Players:**   Two or more.

❑ **Game Plan:** The first player begins by looking at the letters on a license plate and using those letters in that order to begin a story. Example: For a license plate that has the letters G, L, and D, the player could say, "Gary Loped to Denver." The next player must keep that theme going, however loosely, with the letters on the next license plate. Example: For a license plate with the letters B and C on it, the next player could add "Being cautious." If the next license plate had the letters F, Y, and N, the following player could say, "Feeling Young, Naturally." Play continues this way.

Note that you should give some leeway in this game. Allowing articles and prepositions that don't match the letters on a plate increases the fun and creativity players can use.

❑ **How To Win:** This is yet another game where the fun is in the playing, not necessarily in competing. However, you can set a time limit and eliminate players if they can't keep the string going within that time frame. As an alternative, cracking up the next player so she can't come up with a line to continue the story is another way to weed out players.

◆

Dissection/Reconstruction

The basic version of the game Dissection calls on players to build words from roadside signs. In Reconstruction, players take turns trying to devise the biggest word possible.

❑ **Aim of the Game:** To take a word from a roadside sign and name as many words as possible from those letters.

❑ **Number of Players:** Two or more.

❑ **Game Plan:** Players take turns choosing a starter word from a roadside sign or some other visible item. The player who selected the starter word begins by naming any sort of word that can be built from the letters in the starter word. The object is not to necessarily come up with the biggest word—any word whose letters all come from the starter word works fine.

Here's an example: Let's say the starter word is Colorado. The first player could begin with "door." The next player must also come up with a word built from the letters in Colorado, such as "cool." The next player must come up with her own word—"color" would be a good choice. Play continues in this fashion as players in turn add to the list of words.

Needless to say, players may not repeat another player's word. It's also a good idea to disallow one-letter words and plural versions of words that have already been suggested.

❑ **How To Win:** Players can be eliminated from the game as they're unable to come up with a new word that works. The last player who identifies a suitable word is the winner.

Dissection is also a great cooperative game, in which players work together to keep the string of words going for as long as possible.

❑ **Variation:** A slightly different way to play is called Reconstruction. Here, the object is to build the biggest word possible from the letters on a roadside sign within a certain time limit. Players take turns selecting a word on a roadside sign or some other visible item. Players have 30 seconds to think of the biggest word they can whose letters all come from the starter word. The order in which the letters first appeared is immaterial—players can move letters as they wish to construct the longest word possible. The players then announce their selections, and the one who comes up with the longest word is the winner.

Here's an example: If the word selected was "Detroit," possible words built from that combination include "rioted" and "trite." Once players announce the words they've devised, play moves on with the selection of another word.

You can also vary scoring in Reconstruction. Rather than just declaring a winner after every word, players add up the letters from each word they construct and keep a running total. The first player to score 50 points is the winner. As an added element, any player who's able to use all the letters in a word receives a 10-point bonus. Additionally, try experimenting with different time limits if 30 seconds seems too fast. However, going past a minute will probably slow the game down too much.

Judy's License Letter Game

Judy thought this up while we were driving home from Washington State's San Juan Island region, although some players may discover they've actually been playing this game for years.

❑ **Aim of the Game:**   To take the letters on a car license plate and use them in a creative phrase.

❑ **Number of Players:**   One or more.

❑ **Game Plan:**   A car passes with the letters *A, B,* and *C* on its license plate. The first player uses those letters to make a phrase in which each word begins with those letters—in this case, a good phrase might be, "All Bohemians Create" or "Alaskans Buy California." The more creative, funny, or personally appropriate the phrase—depending on the wishes of the players—the better. The next player then takes his or her turn, and so on through all the players in the car.

❑ **How To Win:**   This game need not have a winner, as the fun of the game is to see what players can create with various letter combinations. If a winner is desired, however, players can agree beforehand to choose which player creates the best combination from each license plate.

❑ **Variations:** For one spinoff, players must create a phrase having to do with the state listed on that particular license plate. For instance, with the *A, B,* and *C* example listed above, a player seeing the combination on a Connecticut license plate would have to come up with something like, "Always Buy Connecticut." Similarly, "Absolutely Beautiful Cambridge" would be one good possibility for a Massachusetts plate.

Think people look like their dogs? You'll be astounded when you start to notice the similarity between people and their license plates. The aim of this variation is to take license plate letters and create what you would think would be a fitting name for or descriptive phrase about the driver (or a passenger) of that particular car. Using our *A, B,* and *C* example, a fitting phrase for a tyke riding in an expansive luxury car might be "a budding capitalist." Is Dad alongside junior, ready for battle in his three-piece, busy cutting deals on his cellular phone? That could well be "Amory Bountiful Cashflow."

Letter Juggle

This game suggests a juggler who's busy keeping a bunch of balls in the air while a trusty assistant tosses new ones into the mix. Letter Juggle does this with words, with letters supplied from license plates.

❑ **Aim of the Game:** To build words using an ever-increasing number of letters found on automobile license plates.

❏ **Number of Players:**   Two or more.

❏ **Game Plan:**   This example addresses a two-player game. The game starts with one player finding three letters from a nearby license plate. The other player must then use those three letters in a word. The first player finds one more letter on a license plate—the second player must then use all four letters in a brand-new word. The first player then finds a fifth letter and so on, with the second player continually building new words based on the letters provided.

Here's an example: If the first player found the letters *A, B,* and *C,* the second player could say "abacus." If the next letter was an *N,* the second player could then say "cabana." If the following letter were an *R,* "branch" would be one suitable answer.

   Note: If there are more than two players, players take turns finding additional letters for the player whose turn it is to build words.

   Play continues until a player can no longer come up with a word with the letters supplied. The remaining players then take their turns.

❏ **How To Win:**   Players add up the number of times they were able to think up a word—the player with the greatest number wins. Alternatively, players add up the number of letters of the words they were able to devise—this is best done at the end of each player's turn, not at the end of the round.

❏ **Variations:**   There are several different ways to play Letter Juggle. One thing to consider is some sort of time limit for each word—say thirty seconds or a minute. Another twist that makes the game much more challenging requires players to come up with words that have the letters in the order in which they were found. As such, in the above example, "abacus" would have been an acceptable first word, but the addition of the letter *N* would have required another word, such as "abscond." You may want a more liberal time policy for this version, since it's considerably more demanding.

License To Letter

The structure of License To Letter offers the basis for an array of entertaining, challenging games—particularly for solo players. For a related game that's different enough to stand on its own, be sure to check out Letter Juggle.

❏ **Aim of the Game:**   To build words using license plate letters.

❏ **Number of Players:**   One or more.

❏ **Game Plan:**   The first player chooses a nearby car and reads off the letters on the license plate. That player must then use all those letters in as long a word as possible. For instance, "cab" would be one obvious word choice for a plate with the letters *A, B,* and *C.* However, with some more thought, that player might come up with a word such as "beach" or "baccalaureate."

One point is assigned for each letter in the word. The next player then takes his turn with the same license plate, adding up the number of points contained in his word.

❑ **How To Win:**   While players may wish to continue play without having a target point total in mind, setting a winning total—say, 50 points—can add an edge of competition to a game. Single players can set a target goal and see how many words it takes them to reach that goal.

❑ **Variations:**   There are several different ways to play this game. For instance, one interesting variant calls on players to take letters and use them in two words that somehow go together. This make the game somewhat easier—you're not required to fit a bunch of letters into one word—while also making it more difficult, since you've got to come up with two words instead of one.

Example: with the license plate *A, B, C,* one possibility might be "taxi cab." This version is scored the same as the main version, with one point being assigned for each letter.

Want to make this variant even more difficult? Try it with vanity plates.

Memory Games

"Memory, the warder of the brain."

—*Shakespeare*

Carry Over

This game is similar to others in which players start and continue with sentences. In this case, however, there's a significant and entertaining difference.

❏ **Aim of the Game:**   To build a sentence in which each word starts with the last letter of the prior word.

❏ **Number of Players:**   One or more.

❏ **Game Plan:**   The first player starts the game by naming a word. The next player must then add another word that begins with the last letter of the first word. The next player must add a third word that begins with the last letter of the second word, and so on. The trick is to begin and to continue building a sentence as you go along—as such, every word that's added must somehow make sense.

Example: The first player starts with the word "I"—with one-letter words, that letter must begin the next word. The second player adds the word "investigated." Following the sequence, the next player must add a word beginning with *D*—"doing" might be one such word.

   Players continue to add on words in this way. Before a player may add on a word, he must repeat the sentence to that point. Here's how our example might turn out after a few more turns: "I investigated doing gorgeous, special landscaping, grabbing George's shears so other rambunctious snoops stopped dawdling."

Proper nouns and possessives are permitted in Carry Over, as was the case in the above example with "George's." In that instance, the next player's word had to start with *S*. In addition, once a string of words reaches a point where it can become a sentence, the player whose turn it is may declare that sentence complete and begin a new sentence—however, should the player wish to continue, he may simply add on an appropriate word. Both instances happened in our example: after "landscaping," the player chose "grabbing," while the player whose turn came after "dawdling" ended the sentence.

❑ **How To Win:**   This is a game that is entertaining enough without competition. However, players may be eliminated if they're unable to add a word that either begins with the last letter of the prior word or if they suggest a word the other players feel makes no sense. Players can also be dropped if they can't repeat the entire sentence. Adding a time limit gives the competitive game an additional twist.

Conga Line

The challenge here is to remember words in a particular series while adding to the sequence. Thus, Conga Line is a test of both memory and creativity.

❑ **Aim of the Game:**   To keep adding words to an alphabetical category of words.

❏ **Number of Players:**   Two or more.

❏ **Game Plan:**   Before starting, players agree on some sort of relatively broad category, such as cities, movies, animals, celebrities, or some other large grouping. From there, the first player names a word that fits the category that begins with the letter *A*. The next player repeats that word, then adds an appropriate word beginning with the letter *B*. The next player repeats the *A* and *B* words, then contributes a word beginning with *C*, and so on.

Example: With the category of actors, the first player can start by saying "Don Ameche." The next player can then say, "Don Ameche, Gary Busey." The third player can then add, "Don Ameche, Gary Busey, Tom Cruise." (Note that, for people, the first letter of the last name is the one that counts.)

❏ **How To Win:**   Players are eliminated if they either cannot remember all the prior words in the conga line or if they're unable to come up with an addition that fits both the category and the letter with which they must start. The last player to successfully do both is the winner.

❏ **Variation:**   One offshoot of Conga Line is Nadas. In this more challenging version, letters which players miss during the game are identified as "nadas," a label which the other players must remember and identify as play continues. For instance, let's say a player in the example above missed the *D* word. The next player would be required to repeat the following: "Don Ameche, Gary Busey, Tom Cruise, nada," before adding any word beginning with *E* that fits the category.

Each subsequent player would have to remember that "nada," as well as any others that might result from players' misses.

Embellish

This is a well-known party game that's also fun to play on the road. We've included a variation to give a different slant to this entertaining test of recall and imagination.

❏ **Aim of the Game:**   To remember and build on a sentence.

❏ **Number of Players:**   Two or more.

❏ **Game Plan:**   One player starts the game by naming an object. The next player adds a descriptive word or brief phrase that builds on the initial word. The next player then repeats what has been formed so far, adding something of her own to the sentence.

Example: The first player starts by saying, "A book." The next players says, "A gray book." The player after that says, "A torn, gray book." The next player may then add a bit more to the sentence: "A torn, gray book on a couch," and so on.

So long as they remember what has been said up to that point, players may add whatever they wish to make the sentence grow longer. The only rule is that each addition should be limited to a few words at most. Taking the above example a few steps farther, the sentence may sound like "A torn, gray book on a dusty couch against the drafty window that looks out on the leafy, windswept lawn . . ."

❑ **How To Win:** Players drop out of the game when they can no longer repeat the entire sentence and add something onto it. The winner is the last player to successfully do so.

❑ **Variation:** In Alliterative Embellish, players may only add words that begin with the same letter—every noun, adjective, verb, and other significant word in the sentence must begin with the same letter. Turning the above example into an alliterative one, the sentence might look like: "A brown, bawdy book on a bouncing bed in a billowy boudoir that betrays blustery, bellicose beings." (Articles and prepositions need not share the same first letter.)

Itinerary

This game tests both your memory and your knowledge of geography.

❑ **Aim of the Game:** To list a series of places in which each location starts with the last letter of the prior place.

❑ **Number of Players:** One or more.

❑ **Game Plan:** One player starts the game by saying, "I'm going on a trip to . . ." and completes the sentence by naming a place—in this case, let's say "Alaska." The next player must repeat that, then add a destination that begins with *A*—"I'm going on a trip to Alaska and then to Albany." The next player repeats, then adds a word with the letter *Y*—"I'm going on a trip to Alaska, then to Albany, then to

Yuma." Players who can't recall the whole string and add something new drop out.

❑ **How To Win:** The last player to successfully repeat the entire series of places is the winner.

Singing and Rhyming Games

"That which is not worth speaking,
they can sing."

—Beaumarchais

Add Versity

With apologies to Shakespeare, who is probably and justifiably car-oming off the walls of his grave right about now, poetry-based games can prove to be entertaining travel fare.

❏ **Aim of the Game:** To start and add to a rhyming poem.

❏ **Number of Players:** One or more.

❏ **Game Plan:** The first player begins the poem by reciting a line he has devised. The next player must continue the poem by rhyming a new line with the first line. Players continue this rhyming scheme as long as they can.

As an example, the first player starts by saying, "On Monday I took my vacation." The second player may build on that by saying, "By bringing my bags to the station." The third player may choose to add, "I wanted some information," which might be followed by, "To avoid holiday consternation," and so on.

Players who are unable to add a line drop out of the game.

❏ **How To Win:** The last player to successfully add a line to the poem is declared the winner. Alternately, players may choose not to declare a winner, merely enjoying each others' creativity and trying to keep the poem alive as long as possible.

❑ **Suggestions For Play:**   Although the idea in competitive Add Versity is to stump the other players, the best games occur when the first player starts with a word that's easy enough to rhyme, such as "vacation" in the above example. Keep in mind that even the easiest of rhyming words will become tough once the possibilities begin to dwindle. The game can be made even more challenging if players agree that every line must make some sort of sense.

Chain Singing

This game was suggested by our friend Nan Gatchel, who used to play it while taking car trips to various exotic destinations in Ohio. It's a simple game, but getting folks to sing never fails to entertain.

❑ **Aim of the Game:**   To sing a line or two from a song, stopping at a particular word. The next player sings another song, somehow using the last word sung by the prior player.

❑ **Number of Players:**   Two or more.

❑ **Game Plan:**   The first player starts the game by singing a line or two from a song. In choosing the song, the player thinks of a word in the song that is a prominent word in another song—the player ends her song on that word. The next player must sing another song that uses that last word. The second player need not sing the song the first player had in mind, but one that uses the last word in some way.

As an example, the first player starts off the game in true sporting fashion by singing "Oh, say can you see, by the dawn's early light" and stops there, thinking of the song "You Light Up My Life." However, the second player takes a somewhat different tack: "Come on baby, light my fire . . . try to set the night on fire" and stops there—in this case, the player has the song "Fire on the Mountain" in mind. The next player must then come up with a song to sing that somehow uses the word "fire," and play continues in this fashion.

Players who break the chain when they cannot come up with a song are eliminated from play. When someone is unable to name another song, the prior player must sing the song he had in mind from the last clue. That player then comes up with a line or two from a new song, and play goes on.

Another way to weed players out of a game is through challenges. If a player thinks that the prior player did not have a song in mind when finishing a turn, she may challenge the first player to sing the song. Players who are caught bluffing are eliminated from the game. However, any player who challenges another unsuccessfully is also dropped from the game.

❏ **How To Win:**   The last player to successfully sing a song is the winner.

❏ **Suggestions For Play:**   Similar to other games, this one may involve titles with which everyone might not be all that familiar, such as obscure alma maters and local television advertising jingles seemingly conceived in an ether-induced funk. Before beginning play, establish that an acceptable song is one that most or all of the players will recognize.

Limerick Logistics

This enjoyable and challenging game combines travel with the ancient art of devising limericks.

❑ **Aim of the Game:**   To use towns, cities, and other locations in a limerick.

❑ **Number of Players:**   One or more.

❑ **Game Plan:**   Players decide who goes first. Those players waiting for their turn look for a road sign or some other visible item and pick out a town, city, village, or any other name that appears. The player whose turn it is must use that name in a five-line limerick.

As an example, let's say the players have picked out the name "Seattle." Here's one way that might be used:

> *There once was a man from Seattle*
> *whose career was a lifelong battle*
> *his employer, a chump,*
> *deserved a boot in the rump*
> *from the people he treated like cattle.*

Play then passes to the next player, who is then given his word from the other players.

❑ **How To Win:**   This game need not have a winner, as play can be perfectly entertaining unto itself. However, after a round players have the option of choosing the most clever, poignant, pertinent—whatever—limerick.

❏ **Suggestions For Play:** This is a good game in which to set a time limit. The constraint of time often produces some of the best limericks. But try to be reasonable.

❏ **Variations:** One variant to this game is to have all the players use the same word to form their limericks. The game becomes more challenging as play progresses and possibilities dwindle.

Another possibility is to have players come up with towns and cities from memory, rather than reading them from road signs. Yet another option is using a road atlas. The object here would be to find places whose names would be particularly difficult to use in a limerick. (Just try slipping Lake Wonoskopomuc into one.)

No No

This unique game tests your ability to decipher a clue, then devise a suitable rhyme.

❏ **Aim of the Game:** To start and maintain a series of rhyming words.

❏ **Number of Players:** Two or more.

❏ **Game Plan:** The first player starts the game by naming a word, then adds a definition that suggests a word that rhymes with the first word. The next player must say "No, No," identify the word the first player suggested with the definition, and then offer another definition that suggests another word that rhymes with the first two words.

Here is, no doubt, a much-needed example. Let's say the first player starts a game by saying the word "cake," then adds a definition that suggests a word that rhymes with cake. One possibility here would be: "A cake is something you gather leaves with." If the next player understands that clue, he would answer, "No, no, you mean rake, which is where you go fishing." From there, the next player might say, "No, no, you mean lake, which is the opposite of give." The next player would likely catch on to the clue for "take" and play would continue from there.

❑ **How To Win:** Players are eliminated if they are unable to decipher a definition that is given to them. Players are also knocked out if they can't think of another word that rhymes with the string.

Miscellaneous Games

"No pleasure lasts long unless there is variety in it."

—*Publilius Syrus*

Alliti-List

We based this game on a speech pathology test that measures organizational ability. Taken a few steps beyond that, Alliti-List is great for solo as well as competitive play. Simple it may be, but easy it's not.

❏ **Aim of the Game:** To name as many things as possible that begin with the same letter and also match a predetermined category. The game is timed.

❏ **Number of Players:** One or more.

❏ **Game Plan:** Our example addresses a two-player game. The players agree on a category—let's say musicians. One player chooses a letter for the other player, who then has one minute to name all the musicians she can think of whose names begin with that letter. Once she's done, she chooses a letter for the first player, who also has one minute to name all the musicians he can think of that match that letter. Players get one point for each name.

Here's an example: Using the musicians category, one player gives the other player the letter *C*. Here's a sample of the answers she could come up with: Chopin, Harry Chapin, Cab Calloway, Commander Cody—you get the idea.

This player then gives the first player the letter *M*. Here are some possibilities: Mozart, Montovani, Glenn Miller, Steve Miller (same last name but different guys), Milli Vanilli (this would probably count as an *M* name, although calling them musicians is rather generous).

❑ **How To Win:** Players time each other and add up their scores. The largest number wins.

❑ **Variations:** Two ways to vary the game involve choice of letters and the way games are timed. Instead of having players choose letters for other players, letters can be chosen at random from license plates or signs—agreeing to use the first letter on the next license plate you see adds a greater element of chance to a game. Additionally, rather than using a watch to time a turn, try a car odometer. Have players' turns last for a mile or so.

Another variation has players taking turns with the same letter. As such, in the first example we gave, the first player might say Chick Corea, then the next player would also have to think of a musician whose name begins with *C,* such as Harry Connick Jr. Players are dropped from the game when they can't come up with an answer to keep the string of names alive.

This is also a great solo game. Pick a category, select a word, and give yourself a minute (or a mile) to list everything you can think of. It's surprisingly diverting.

Lastly, don't limit yourself to only a few categories—foods, geographic locations, and other like subjects are also suited to Alliti-List. The rule of thumb is that a category should be broad enough to provide a reasonable number of possibilities.

Assembly

Players match their word association skills in this game of quick thinking and ingenuity.

❑ **Aim of the Game:**   To build as short a sentence as possible with words supplied by various players.

❑ **Number of Players:**   Two or more.

❑ **Game Plan:**   Players suggest five words to be used for that particular round. The five words must include a noun (either a person or a thing), a place, a verb, an adjective, and an adverb. In turn, players suggest words that fit each category in that order. Then the first player must make up as short a sentence as possible using all five words.

Here's an example. Players suggest the following words: penguin, Mars, tap dance, verbose, sexually. The first player might assemble something along the following lines: "A sexually active penguin, who was too verbose, was sentenced to Mars where he spent his life tap dancing." From there, players count the number of words a player used and play moves on with the next player taking those same five words and assembling a sentence.

No player may copy another's sentence. Additionally, players' sentences must make some sense. The above example, while certainly far-fetched, does have some reason to it. To make things fair, players should alternate who goes first.

❏ **How To Win:**   At the end of a round, the player who used the fewest number of words in her sentence is the winner.

❏ **Suggestions For Play:**   This is one game where a time limit of some sort would be a good idea. This constraint not only prompts players to think quickly, but the results produced under a fast deadline can often be hilarious, to say the least.

❏ **Variation:**   Rather than counting the number of words used, players may decide who used all five words in the most creative way. In this variation, ingenuity, not merely the size of the sentence, becomes the most important consideration.

Categories

This is our version of a well-known game that usually involves pencil and paper. We've come up with a way to play that doesn't require any equipment.

❏ **Aim of the Game:**   To name a series of words within four specified categories.

❏ **Number of Players:**   Two or more.

❏ **Game Plan:**   Players should imagine a grid with four categories running along the top and four letters along the side. The object is to "fill" the grid by naming things in a category that start with the various letters—in our version, those letters are the first four letters of each player's name.

Here's an example. Say Jennifer is the first player. She chooses the four categories for that round: books, sports teams, actors, and foods. She starts the round by naming a book that starts with *J*, the first letter of her name: *Jitterbug Perfume*. Then the next player names a book beginning with a *J*, and so on until all players have taken their turn. Players then move on to *E*, each naming a book beginning with that letter. Following that, players take two rounds with the letter *N* (since those are the third and fourth letters in her name). Once the books category is finished, play moves on to the next category and follows the same pattern of play.

   The game is finished when the first four letters in Jennifer's name have been played in all four categories. A new game can then be started with another player's name. He names four categories and play begins with the first category and the first letter of his name.

❑ **How To Win:**   The winner is the player with the fewest number of misses.

Coming and Going

This alphabet-based game requires players to pay attention to both ends of their words. This is also a good game for solo play.

❑ **Aim of the Game:**   To start and continue an alphabetical series of words in which both the first and last letters are the same.

❑ **Number of Players:**   One or more.

❑ **Game Plan:**   This is a simple one. The first player takes the letter *A* and thinks of a word that begins and ends with that letter, such as "amoeba." The next player does the same with *B*—"bomb." The next player follows suit with *C*, and so on. (As with other alphabet-based games, you may wish to skip *Q, X,* and *Z*, since those letters offer sparse possibilities).

❑ **How To Win:**   Players drop from the game when they're unable to come up with a suitable word. The last player remaining is the winner.

❑ **Variations:**   One way to make things more challenging is to stipulate word length. For instance, players can specify that all words have to be five letters long. Needless to say, that makes the game a good deal more difficult.

Another way to play is to keep the basic game, but players must take turns to see how far they each can get through the alphabet within a certain time limit. The player who's able to name the most words is the winner.

Yet another variation has players taking turns with the same letter. The game begins with the first player thinking of a word that begins and ends with an *A*—the remaining players must do the same in turn. The players then proceed to *B* and so on. Players can either be eliminated on their first miss or, to make the game a bit more competitive, players have to accumulate five misses before they're dropped from the game. Be sure to rotate who goes first with each letter—that way, no one player always has the disadvantage of having to think of a suitable word after other players have already done so. The game becomes even more challenging if all the words have to be the same length.

Grill 'Em

We first noticed this simple yet entertaining game in Tom Stoppard's play Rosencrantz and Guildenstern Are Dead. *Any questions?*

❑ **Aim of the Game:**   To keep a conversation going using only questions.

❑ **Number of Players:**   Two or more.

❑ **Game Plan:**   This is easy. The first player starts by asking a question of another player, who answers with another question. This is answered with yet another question, and so on. However loosely, a question should have some sort of logical relationship to the prior question.

Here's a sample exchange:
- **Player #1:**   How are you today?
- **Player #2:**   What's it to you?
- **Player #3:**   Isn't he in a bad mood?
- **Player #1:**   Did I ask you to interrupt?
- **Player #2:**   Why do you ask?
- **Player #3:**   Are you trying to make sense of this?

This is one game where players should answer within a certain amount of time—say, 15 seconds or so. Time constraints add to the challenge of the game.

❏ **How To Win:** Players are eliminated as they're unable to come up with a question to keep the game going. Players are also dropped from a game if they accidentally make some sort of statement or repeat a prior question.

By the way, the two ill-fated messengers from Hamlet didn't allow any rhetoric in their game. However, they were put to death at the end of the play, so that's a good enough reason for us to permit such statements as, "What in God's name is going on?" and other like questions. Life's too short.

Oh, Skip It

As the name suggests, this game calls on players to list words in which vowels and consonants alternate. Challenging for both multi-player games as well as solo play.

❏ **Aim of the Game:** To build an alphabetical list of words in which vowels and consonants alternate.

❏ **Number of Players:** One or more.

❏ **Game Plan:** The basic game involves four-letter words. The first player starts by naming a word that begins with the letter *A*, has a consonant for the second letter, a vowel for the third letter, and ends with a consonant. One possibility is "abut." The next player must think of a word that starts with the letter *B*, has a second letter that's a vowel, a third letter that's a consonant, and whose final letter is a vowel—how about "bile." This pattern holds for a word beginning with *C,* such as "cola."

Play continues in this fashion through the alphabet, with the first letter of the word dictating the pattern that the remainder of the word must follow.

❑ **How To Win:** Any player who cannot come up with a suitable word drops out of the game. The last player remaining is the winner.

❑ **Suggestions For Play:** Like other games, this is one where it's impossible to come up with a suitable word that begins with *Q* and *X*. Unless you're hungry for a cutthroat game where it's a simple matter of bad luck for players to be eliminated, you may want to skip these letters.

❑ **Variations:** Naturally enough, Oh, Skip It becomes more challenging the longer the words get. Try moving up to five-letter words and see how that goes.

A multiplayer variation requires players to start their words with the last letter from the prior word. For example, if one player started a game with the word "abut," the next player's word would have to start with a *T*—"take" would be one example. Since this version eliminates the predictability of alphabetical order, it doesn't allow players the luxury of planning ahead for their next word.

Verboten

Where many games call on you to include certain letters, this one requires that you leave some out.

❑ **Aim of the Game:**   To answer questions from other players, omitting specified letters from your answer.

❑ **Number of Players:**   Two or more.

❑ **Game Plan:**   The rules are simple. In turn, players ask each other questions and specify two letters the responding player may not use in her answer. The player who answers must use at least three words, thereby omitting easy one-word replies.

Here's an example. One player asks another, "How were things at work today?" then adds "*S* and *T*"—the two letters the responding player may not use in her answer. Here's a good reply: "Fairly good, really." If the player's answer was appropriate, as it was in this case, another player then asks another question: "Are you expecting a raise soon? *M* and *A*," to which one suitable answer would be, "Not in the next few weeks."

Verboten is one game where a player should have a short time limit in which to devise an answer, say, 15 to 30 seconds. While that may seem like the third degree—players verbally surrounding and peppering another player with questions he's got to answer at once—it also offers an entertaining, quick-thinking exercise.

❏ **How To Win:** A player continues until she misses a question. Other players take their turns, and the one who fields the most questions correctly is the winner.

❏ **Variations:** One way to make Verboten even more of a challenge is to increase the number of "forbidden" letters to three. Another variant has players asking questions back and forth rather than having one player answer question after question. Here's how a sample exchange from that game might look:

- **Player #1 (to #2):** "How's it going today? *F* and *G*."
- **Player #2:** "I'm very well, thank you." (To #3): "How's everything by you? *S* and *N*."
- **Player #3:** I'm good, how thoughtful of you to query." (To #1): "Have you gotten over your flu yet? *R* and *A*."
- **Player #1:** Yes, but not my cough."

Again, the key to a good game of Verboten is to keep things moving so that players have to think on their feet. That often leads to players talking answers out loud as they're devising them, which can produce entertaining results.

Reader Response

Have any suggestions on how these games could be improved? Got any games that you'd like to suggest for a future collection? Anyone who submits a game that we use will be credited. Please send us a letter with your feedback or new game idea, and be sure to include the following information: name, address, and a telephone number. Thanks!

Jeff and Judy Wuorio
2822 South West Carolina St.
Portland, OR 97201